The Ladybird Key Words Reading Scheme is based on these commonly used words. Those used most often in the English language are introduced first—with other words of popular appeal to children. All the Key Words list is covered in the early books, and the later titles use further word lists to develop full reading fluency. The total number of different words which will be learned in the complete reading scheme is nearly two thousand. The gradual introduction of these words, frequent repetition and complete 'carry-over' from book to book, will ensure rapid learning.

The full colour illustrations have been designed to create a desirable attitude towards learning — by making every child *eager* to read each title. Thus this attractive reading scheme embraces not only the latest findings in word frequency, but also the natural interests and activities of happy children.

Each book contains a list of the new words introduced.

W MURRAY, the author of the Ladybird Key Words Reading Scheme, is an experienced headmaster, author and lecturer on the teaching (*with J McNally, of* Key Word *book published by The Teach*

D0528353

THE LADYBIRD KEY WORDS READING SCHEME has 12 graded books in each of its three series—'**a**', '**b**' and '**c**'. These 36 graded books are all written on a controlled vocabulary, and take the learner from the earliest stages of reading to reading fluency.

The '**a**' series gradually introduces and repeats new words. The parallel '**b**' series gives the needed further repetition of these words at each stage, but in a different context and with different illustrations.

The '**c**' series is also parallel to the '**a**' series, and supplies the necessary link with writing and phonic training.

An illustrated booklet—*Notes for using the Ladybird Key Words Reading Scheme*—can be obtained free from the publishers. This booklet fully explains the Key Words principle. It also includes information on the reading books, work books and apparatus available, and such details as the vocabulary loading and reading ages of all books.

Published by Ladybird Books Ltd Loughborough Leicestershire UK
Ladybird Books Inc Auburn Maine 04210 USA

Printed in England

BOOK 1a
The Ladybird Key Words Reading Scheme

Play with us

by W MURRAY
with illustrations by J H WINGFIELD

Ladybird Books

Peter   Jane

a dog   a tree   a ball

toys   a shop

Peter

Jane

a dog a tree a ball

toys a shop

Peter

---

new word

Peter

Jane

Jane

Peter and Jane

---

new word

and

here is Peter

and

here is Jane

new words   here   is

Peter is here

and

Jane is here.

Here is

the dog.

Here is Jane and here is the dog.

Jane likes
the dog
and
Peter likes
the dog.

---

new word

likes

The dog
likes Jane
and
the dog
likes Peter.

The

I like Peter.

I like Jane.

I like

the dog.

Here is a shop.

a shop

Here is

a toy shop.

I like

the toy shop.

Peter is in

the toy shop.

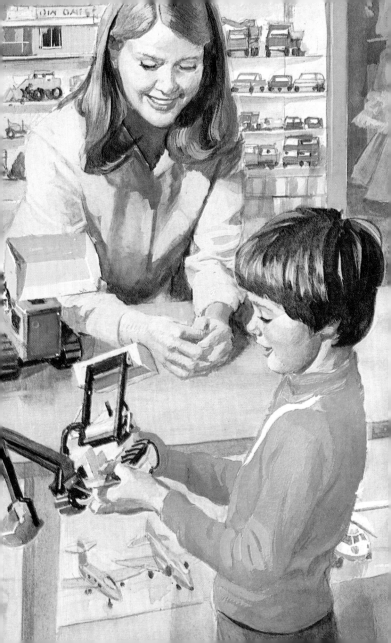

Jane is in

the toy shop.

The dog is in
the toy shop.

Peter has a toy

and

Jane has a toy.

---

new word   has

Peter has a ball.

Peter likes

the ball.

---

new word

ball

Here is the dog.
The dog has
the ball.

Here is a tree.

The ball is in

the tree.

Peter is in the tree and Jane is in the tree.

Here is Peter
in the tree.
Peter has
the ball.

Words used in this book

Total number of words 16

Now read book 1b